Miniature Pigs as Pets

The Ultimate Guide for Miniature Pigs

Miniature Pigs Breeding, Buying, Care, Cost, Keeping, Health, Supplies, Food, Rescue and More Included!

By Lolly Brown

Foreword

Miniature Pigs are carefully bred and developed by researchers because they simply need a pig that is much more manageable than the normal huge – sized breed. Although pigs had been around for hundreds of years, the newly developed mini pigs only came about around the 1960's. Miniature pigs came from different hog's species that were genetically selected to produce a smaller version of it. Eventually because of their adorable and manageable characteristic, some people made them as pets.

Although mini pigs are truly a great choice as pets, these animals doesn't come with a thin instruction manual, but fear not! In this book you'll be easily guided on understanding your mini pigs; their behaviors, their characteristics, how you should feed and care for them and a whole lot more.

Embark on a wonderful journey of sharing your life with mini pigs. Learn to maximize the great privilege of living with one and be able to share this unique and unforgettable experience just like many pet pig owners that came before you!

Table of Contents

Introduction

Miniature pigs are the cute and manageable version of the hog world; they are also known as mini pigs obviously because of their small size. People liked them as pets because of their great personality and simply because it's a unique choice. Mini pigs are fairly young breed of animals; it was developed and carefully selected in United States by researchers around the 1950's to 1960's because they wanted to study the hog creature but soon realized that these animals grow very fast and huge, so developing a mini pig is a much more manageable option. Overtime a wide variety of mini pigs became popular as pets because it's unique and oh – so adorable! It can be a farm pet and even a house pet, these creatures are also eligible for "mini pig fashion shows." Mini pigs have a docile personality that you can never get in the wild. But what is it that makes these pet so popular? There is no short answer to this question because, with Miniature pigs, there is just so much to love.

The mini pigs are more than just a pet; it is a friendly, active and also an interesting companion much like dogs and cats. These pigs are quite trainable, cuddly and energetic, plus they are also very great family pets, although they may not be ideal for very young children. If you are thinking about rescuing or purchasing a mini pig, there are many types of breed you can choose from.

Before you bring a mini pig home, however, you should be a responsible pet pig owner and learn everything you can about this breed and how to care for it properly.

Fortunately, this ultimate guide will teach you on how to be the best miniature pig owner you can be! Inside this book, you will find tons of helpful information about different types of mini pigs; how they live, how to deal with them and realize the great benefits of owning one!

This book includes information about creating the ideal habitat and diet for your rabbit as well as tips for breeding and showing your mini pigs. You will also find in-depth health information for the breed including common health problems affecting it and the treatment options available.

The fluffy world of miniature pig awaits! Get ready for a wild mini hog adventure!

Glossary of Mini Pig Terms

Abscess: A pocket of infection under the skin filled with pus. You May need veterinary care.

Adult teeth: The final set of teeth of a pig, after the baby teeth have fallen out.

American Mini Pig: Pet pig of mixed breed heritage fitting the American Mini Pig Breed Standard and registered by the American Mini Pig Association Registry.

Anesthetics: Medications or drugs that cause reversible loss of sensation, anesthesia. These medications are either gas or injection. Anesthetics are used to put a pig "under" for surgery or other medical procedures. Common anesthetics in pigs are Isoflorane gas or ISO gas, Ketamine, Xylazine, Telazol, and Propofol.

Anthelmintic: Anti parasite medication, dewormers. Examples are Ivomec (Ivermectin) and SafeGuard (Fenbendazole)

Antibiotics: Medications or drugs to treat bacterial infections.

Arthritis: Joint pain or joint disease usually associated with advanced age.

Atrophic Rhinitis (AR): A serious disease in pigs due to the bacteria Pasteurella multocidia. Atrophic Rhinitis affects the naval passage with sneezing, drainage, and eventual deformity.

Baby teeth: Teeth of a piglet or young pig that will fall out as the mature teeth come in. The teeth of a newborn pig are called needle teeth or milk teeth.

Barrow: Male pig that was castrated before sexual maturity.

Biosecurity: Procedures or actions taken to prevent the spread of disease.

Blowing Coat: A seasonal change in coat where pigs shed their hair before growing in a new coat of hair.

Boar: Intact male pig, not neutered.

Boar Musk: A highly offensive odor produced by intact boar pigs fueled by testosterone.

Body Condition Score: A numeric score to describe the range of body condition in a mini pig. 1 and 2 show the body of an underweight pig, 3 shows a healthy weight pig, 4 and 5 show the body of an overweight or obese pig.

Body Temperature: The normal body temperature of a mini pig is 99 – 101 degrees.

Brucellosis: A zoonotic bacterial infection. Pigs are suspeptible to brucellosis and can transmit the disease to humans.

Bulk: In the pig's diet, bulk is fiber or filling foods.

Castration: To neuter a mini pig.

Coccidiosis: AKA Coccidia. A parasitic disease of the intestinal tract of animals caused by coccidian protozoa. Causes dangerous diarrhea especially in young piglets.

Colostrum: First milk produced by the sow with each litter of piglets. Very valuable nutrients providing immunity to piglets for the first several weeks.

Conjunctivitis: Infection in the eye.

Constipation: Condition of hardened stools making it difficult to eliminate.

Contagious: A disease or infection that can be transmitted to another person or animal.

Cryptorchidism: A hereditary condition in which one or both testicles failed to descend into the scrotum. A neuter will require abdominal surgery to retrieve the undescended testicle.

Declaws: The two smaller, non-weight bearing toes on each hoof.

Dippity Pig: Dippity Pig Syndrome is an acute, painful skin condition that occurs along the back in healthy young pigs. AKA Bleeding Back Syndrome or Erythema Multiforme.

Enrichment: Animal enrichment is the process of providing a stimulating environment for your pet. Enrichment is described as improving or enhancing the environment to provide an outlet for natural behaviors and needs through physical and mental challenges. These types of enrichment are used by zoos, sanctuaries, and pet owners worldwide.

Entropian: A hereditary condition in which a portion of the eyelid is folded inward. This can cause the eyelashes to irritate and scratch the surface of the eye resulting in pain, infections, scarring, and eventual blindness.

Erysipelas: AKA Diamond Back Disease A bacterial skin infection that is deadly to pigs if not treated early. Signs include high fever, lack of appetite, lethargy, and in some cases skin welts.

Euthanasia: To humanely end the life of a pet in order to stop irreversible suffering.

External Parasites: Parasites that live on the outside of a pig's body, most commonly mites, swine lice, and ticks.

Farrowing Pen: A secure area to provide care for the sow before and after birthing by allowing her to get individual food, water, and care. The farrowing pen also protects piglets after farrowing as it prevents the sow from squashing the piglets. Piglets need higher temperatures than sows so pens allow a separate area for piglets to keep warm.

Farrowing: When a sow gives birth to piglets.

Fecal: A test done by the veterinarian to check stool for signs of parasites.

Flop: The act of a pig flopping onto its side. They usually do this in response to being "forked" or wanting a belly rub.

Forking: The act of poking a pig with something pointed (such as a fork) to elicit a pleasure response.

Fostering: To temporarily house, love, and provide care to a displaced pet pig until an adoptive home is found.
Foster Failure: A loving reference to adopt the pig that you were meant to be fostering. The "failure" is that you didn't complete the search for an adoptive family, which is a great thing!!

Frothing: Foaming at the mouth. Pigs do this in response to food or sexual arousal.

Geriatric: The life stage of pigs in their elderly years requiring special care.

Gestation: The length of pregnancy. In mini pigs this is 3 months, 3 weeks, and 3 days.

Gilt: A young female pig between being a weaner and her first litter. Once she has her first litter she is called a sow.

Herd: A group or family of pigs.

Hernia: Occurs when the intestines push through a weak spot or tear in the lower abdominal wall causing a visible bulge in the abdomen or testicular area (inguinal).

Hoof: The hard nail on a pig's foot that must be maintained at a proper length through trimming, filing, or natural abrasion.

Hypoglycemia: Low blood sugar, especially dangerous in very young piglets.

Inbreeding: To breed pigs with close family lines.

Inguinal Hernia: A hernia in such case as the intestines protrude through the inguinal canal into the scrotal sac. This is an emergency situation and should be evaluated immediately by a veterinarian.

Inguinal Ring, Inguinal Canal: The opening from the abdomen to the scrotum. This canal or ring needs to be stitched closed during neuter to prevent hernia.
Internal Parasites: Parasites that live inside the body of the pig. They may reside in the stomach, intestines, lungs, or kidney.

Intramuscular Injection: An injection given deep into the muscle tissue.

Iron Deficiency Anemia: Low levels of oxygen carrying red blood cells in the blood. Piglets are born with iron deficiency anemia.

Jowl: The hanging fat on a mini pig's neck.

Leptospirosis: A bacterial infection spread by wildlife. This is a zoonotic disease that pigs can contract and spread to humans. Vaccinations are available.

Litter: All the piglets born to one sow from the same pregnancy.

Mange Mites: AKA Sarcoptic Mites or Scabies. The most common external parasites these itchy mites cause great discomfort and secondary skin infections if left untreated. Ivomec (Ivermectin) will treat and prevent mite outbreaks.

Mastitis: Infection in the mammary glands of a nursing mother pig.

Microchip: A form of permanent identification used in mini pigs and other pets. Required by law for some interstate travels.

Milk Line: A protruding line on a sow's teats showing the swelling of incoming milk.

Mini Pig, Miniature Pig: A general term for pet pigs of

purebred or mixed heritage. Mini Pigs are much smaller than their full size counterparts.

Mohawk: The long hairs on the back of a pig's neck that stand up when they are content, excited, or alarmed.

MTP, Move the Pig: A method of communicating to pigs by moving them as they would treat herd mates.

Mulberry Heart Disease: Fatal disease in pigs caused by a deficiency of vitamin e and/or selenium.

Necropsy: An autopsy performed on a mini pig by a veterinarian to determine cause of death.

Needle teeth: set of 8 very sharp teeth in swine that are usually cut off 1 to 3 day old piglets to prevent injury to other piglets and sow's udder.

Neuter: To remove the testicles of a pig for their health and welfare. This is most often done before 8 weeks old. Pigs need to be neutered to make good family pets.

Nose Ring: A barbaric metal ring that is placed into a pig's nose with the intention of causing pain when they root.

Omnivore: A diet consisting of plant and animal matter. Pigs are omnivores by nature requiring a variety of foods.

Ovariohysterectomy: A spay procedure removing the sex organs of a female mini pig.

OTC – Over the counter medication: Medications that can be purchased "over the counter" at your local drugstore without a veterinary prescription.

Oxytocin: A hormone drug used in veterinary medicine to cause uterine contractions in the farrowing sow.

Pan feeding: Feeding orphaned piglets out of a dish, a pan, or a bowl.

Parasites: An organism living in or on the pig, draining it of nutrients or blood. Examples are mites, lice, ticks, roundworms, tapeworms, and coccidiosis.

Porcine Parvo Infection (PPI): A viral infection affecting the reproductive health of pigs.

Permanent Identification: For the purposes of interstate travel, permanent identification is typically required. The form of permanent identification varies. Microchips are preferable. In rare cases an ear tag is required by law.

Piglet: A baby pig.

Polynesian Pig: Pigs living in Hawaii, both as wild pigs and family pets.

Porcine: A general term to describe anything representing or relating to pigs.

Preputial Diverticulum Ablation: Removal of the preputial diverticulum gland, in order to prevent odors from male pigs.

Preputial Diverticulum: AKA Preputial Gland. A butterfly shaped sac dorsal to the prepuce. There is a single opening leading into the prepuce. This pocket inside the sheath is prone to storing semen, urine, and other fluids that are prime breeding ground for bacteria and odors.

Prescription Medication: A medication that can only be obtained through a pharmacy with a prescription by a veterinarian.
Probiotics: Live bacteria and yeasts that are beneficial to the digestive system.

Prolapse: A condition where the vaginal or rectal tissues slip outside of the body. This is an emergency situation that requires immediate veterinary care.

PSS, Porcine Stress Syndrome: A group of conditions caused by a recessive gene. Often causing sudden death due to an episode of high stress, halothane gas, or unknown cause.

Pyometra: Infection of the uterus. Pyometra is a deadly infection if left untreated.

Quarantine: To separate or restrict movement of mini pigs in order to prevent the spread of potential disease or to allow recovery from illness or medical procedures.

Rectal Thermometer: A thermometer that can be inserted rectally to check the temperature of a pig.

Rescue Organization: An officially recognized organization that rescues displaced pigs, fosters them temporarily, screens adoptive homes and places the rescued pigs in new homes.

Respiratory Infection: A viral or bacterial infection of the respiratory tract. Respiratory infections may be mild or serious requiring veterinary treatment.

Ringworm: A fungal infection on the skin causing circular lesions. This infection can be spread to people or other pets.

Rooting: Rooting is a natural behavior for pigs where the pig uses his snout to push or nudge into something repeatedly.

Runt: The smallest pig in the litter. The runt may be small due to competition for nutrition in the womb or congenital defects and failure to thrive. Runts will often catch up to siblings in size once given the chance, sometimes exceeding the size of siblings.

Salt Toxicity or Salt Poisoning: Salt poisoning occurs due to limited water causing a sodium imbalance in the pig.

Sanctuary Organization: An officially recognized group that rescues pigs with the intention and ability to care for them for life. Sanctuaries may or may not adopt out pigs to approved families.

Sarcoptic Mites: AKA Scabies. The most common external parasites these itchy mites cause great discomfort and secondary skin infections if left untreated. Ivomec (Ivermectin) will treat and prevent mite outbreaks.

Scent Glands: Small holes on the front legs of mini pigs that excretes a cheese like compound which containing pheromones and other semiochemical compounds.

Scours: The most common cause of severe diarrhea caused by E. Coli, usually affecting young piglets. Scours is deadly if left untreated.

Scrotum: The external area of the male genital also known as the scrotal sac.

Sedative: Medications or drugs to calm the nervous system. This relaxes the pig to various degrees reducing stress and allowing for medical procedures. Common sedatives used in pigs are Ketamine, Diazepam, Xylazine, Detomidine, Butophenol, Midazolam, Azaperaone.

Snare: A painful restraint device made of a pole and a metal loop that is placed around the pig's snout. The use of snares in pet pigs is unacceptable.

Snout: The nose of a pig, their most sensitive sense organ with a cartilage disk used for digging.

Sorting board: AKA Pig Board. A solid board used to move pigs from one area to another. Also used to protect oneself against the advances of aggressive pigs.

Sow: A female pig that has given birth to a litter of piglets.

Spay: To remove the female reproductive organs.

Stag: Boar that is castrated after maturity.

Subcutaneous Injection: An injection of medication under the skin.

Swine Pox: Contagious viral infection that affects the skin of pigs. The virus can live in the environment for long periods of time. Frequently spread by lice or mange mites.

Swine: A general term for any type of pig.

Teeth Clipping: To clip the infant needle teeth from a piglet. This is usually done at 1 to 3 days old to prevent injury to the sow or litter mates.

Transmissible Diseases: AKA infection diseases. Diseases that can be passed from one pig to another.

Tusk: The canine teeth of pigs. Each pig has 4 tusks, two on bottom and two on top. These are not rooted as normal teeth but are instead attached to the jaw bone. Made of ivory, tusks cannot be removed safely, but can be trimmed as needed.

Umbilical Hernia: Hernia that occurs due to weakened supportive muscles around the umbilical stump or belly button. This causes the umbilical opening not to close properly and intestines protrude through the intestinal wall to form a bulge where the hernia is.

UTI-Urinary Tract Infection: An infection in the urinary tract requiring veterinary care and prescription antibiotics. This infection can turn serious quickly if left untreated, traveling up to the kidneys.

Vitamins: Supplements given to balance the individual nutritional needs of pigs.

Wallow: A deep water or mud hole used for cooling and skin parasite control.

Water Deprivation: Salt poisoning occurs due to limited water causing a sodium imbalance in the pig.

Weaning: Separating piglet from sow/mother

Weight Estimation: The formula to weigh a pig without a scale is to measure using a measure tape. Girth x Girth x Length / 400 = weight in pounds.

Zoomies: AKA Rodeo Pig. A short burst of excitement when mini pig's run or zoom around, sometimes spinning, bucking or barking.

Zoonotic: Infectious diseases of animals that can be transmitted to humans.

Chapter One: Getting to Know Miniature Pigs

Miniature pigs may often time look like your weird friend, the new kid in school, your unexpected roommate, your playful sibling or that very adorable kid you always wanted. In whatever attitude or mood it appeals, you can expect it to be quite docile and wild at the same time yet very interactive and a cool pet you never thought of having.

Miniature pigs are irresistibly cute but it may not be the right choice for everyone. Before you decide whether or not it might be the right pet for you and your family, you need to learn and invest a significant amount of time in getting to know these animals.

In this chapter you will receive an introduction to the different mini pig breeds including some basic facts and information as well as the history of how it came about. This information, in combination with the practical information about keeping miniature pig in the next chapter, will help you decide if this is the perfect pet companion for you.

Facts about Miniature Pigs

In this section you'll find some interesting fun facts about Miniature pigs, their breed origin, breed types and history.

Miniature pigs are domesticated smaller versions of feral hogs and combinations of different pig breeds that were genetically engineered by researchers. In the United States, mini pigs are also known as the "American Mini," they are just the same with pot belly pigs, although they have been classified as a different group because of certain characteristics that aren't found in American mini pigs. In United Kingdom, researchers and animal enthusiasts referred to it as a "Teacup pig."

The American Mini or miniature pigs in general are a "mixed in" or combination of different breed types of feral hogs. Currently there are no tests to determine their genetic make-up or the exact pig breed/s they came from. However, there are parentage test with only a few recognized breeds or types of swine that are filed out. According to research, many pet owners across the United States don't know and will probably never be interested to know the origin of their pet pigs, but one thing is for sure, their popularity as house pets and in local zoos are increasing.

The mixture of genetic breeds from different hogs found in the wild and from their Asiatic ancestors, resulted in a variety of mini pigs that can be identified through their colors. The pure bred hogs and Asiatic pig breeds brought in the U.S. are color white, black as well as black and white with varying patterns. Today, mini pig owners can choose from a variety of colors such as cream, blue, silver, apricot, strawberry, tangerine, auburn, honey, ash, stone, toffee, champagne, maple, praline, caramel, pecan, chestnut, cinnamon, chocolate mahogany, roan and agouti. You can also choose from its wide variety of markings and patterns such as stripes, spots, ticked, solid, pinto, broken, tricolor, point, tuxedo, belted, saddled and blue butt thanks to scientific breakthroughs. Some breeders and mini pig enthusiasts also bred their own mini pigs thus creating new patterns and mixture of colors but some of it are not officially recognized.

Most American Mini Pigs body type is quite different from pot belly pigs, usually the American Mini can be differentiated because of their thicker coat and they don't have a swayed back feature and little to no pot belly.

Fortunately, unlike their wild hog ancestors, most mini pigs are very docile, and friendly creatures and they can also be trained. Miniature pigs are also fond of chewing plants and farm foods like any other farm bred pets, but be careful because some mini pigs are only advised for a certain type of strict diet. For most people mini pigs are low maintenance and manageable that is why they have been developed in the first place, however the needs of your pet pig can be quite expensive, later in this book we will tackle about the things you need in order to take care of your mini pig. These creatures are mostly gentle and understanding and they are naturally people-oriented.

Proper socialization and training from a young age will help prevent the mini pigs from being aggressive to people. Varieties of miniature pigs do very well as family pets and they can also be good with children – although may not be recommended for very young children.

The mini pig has a small but compact body type. It should weigh below 55 pounds; the heaviest can reached 50

- 55 pounds. They usually have black and bright eyes with sniffy noses as most pigs do.

Like any other pets, mini pigs also have a great deal of energy and needs daily exercise to work off that energy through the toys and random experiences that you can provide. It may not be able to adapt to any kind of environment, but if you raised them properly they can be great house pets. They are generally curious yet controllable indoors as long as they get enough mental and physical stimulation during the day and has proper house training as well as litter training.

The average lifespan for the miniature pig breed is between 12 and 18 years, some mini pigs have a longer lifespan; the breed is quite healthy in general as long as you take care of them properly. Like many pets, however, the mini pigs are prone to health issues such as Dippity Pig Syndrome, UTI, Pig Fever and Intestine Parasitism which will also be tackled in the next few chapters later on in this book.

In terms of grooming, the miniature pigs usually have thick coats but it doesn't necessarily need to be brushed and groomed, however their hoofs and dental health requires a regular check-up.

Different Breeds of Miniature Pigs

In this section, you will learn some of the most popular miniature pigs – their physical characteristics, a snapshot of their origin and other important details you need to consider before acquiring them. Not all of the breeds listed below are suitable for you and some may also not be available in your area, so be sure to read the common facts and also try doing a bit of research if you have selected a pet pig breed. The American Mini has the most variety of colors and patterns.

The American Mini Pig

The American Mini is a combination of different variety of hog and domestic pigs around the world. They are solely bred as house pets and companions. It is the perfect pet pig for mini pig enthusiasts out there. It has a compact body and stands at about 15 – 22 inches, smaller in stature and very suitable for indoor/outdoor activities. They are the healthiest type of miniature pig and according to researchers, it has a great temperament.

Mule Foot Hog Breed

The Mule Foot Hog breed has a small head with a proportionate body size and its eyes have are quite apart from each other. It's not suitable as a pet for those who live in small apartments because it is quite huge, it is much suitable for owners who have a garden or a mini farm area on their backyard.

KuneKune Breed

The KuneKune breed is one of the cute mini pigs you can acquire as a pet. It has inclined ears and its tusk, mouth and teeth are mostly used for foraging and grazing. This mini pig loves to run around and generally healthy. It is suitable for owners with a backyard or play pen.

Juliana Breed

This mini pig is just like an American mini because it is quite small and its body is also colorfully spotted. It is usually compared to that of a feral pig and sometimes a large hog because of its physical characteristics. Its body is lean and it is also very athletic. It is perfect for owners who want some pig craziness around the house.

Yucatan Breed

This breed has an overall weight of an average American Mini and it also loves to run around and move freely. It is also suitable for people who have a backyard or play pen in the house.

Pot – Bellied Pig

The pot - bellied pig is a domesticated breed that has a swayed back and a large pot belly on their body hence the name. There are other types of pot belly pigs and it doesn't only refer to a single breed. It came from different ancestors but mostly originated from the Southeast Eurasian continent. There are about fifteen pot -belly pig breed types as of this writing. Some of the pot – belly pigs breeds may not be suitable for your home, it is highly recommended that you do some research first before acquiring one.

Miniature Pigs Sizes

In this section, you will learn the different standard pig sizes for certain breeds. The information given below is taken from the website of American Mini Pig Association, and is therefore not applicable for other countries. This will help you determine the right choice of pet pig size and its classification and may also come in handy when finding a reputable breeder.

Height Classification

Mini Category 1:	14 inches tall and under
Mini Category 2:	Over 14 inches tall up to 16 inches tall
Mini Category 3:	Over 16 inches tall up to 18 inches tall
Mini Category 4:	Over 18 inches tall up to 20 inches tall

Age Classifications

J	= Juvenile pigs under 16 months of age.
A	= Adolescent pigs 16 months to 5 years of age.
M	= Mature adult pigs 5 years or older.

History of Miniature Pigs

Although having a pig as a house pet is relatively new and unique, domesticated pigs have been around as farm pets for thousands of years.

The need for miniature pig arises when scientists and researchers realized how difficult it is to study these creatures because they grew very quickly and heavily up to an average of 150 to 200 pounds.

For quite some time several experiments have been made to create a small version of the pig because it is more manageable and scientists thought that since pigs are anatomically and physically similar to humans they can create a miniature version of it with a couple of specific characteristics engineered to benefit and further their research.

Around the early 1950's, researchers selected different breeds of domesticated pigs and feral hogs and combine it's genetic structure and physical characteristics such as colors, size and growth rates to achieve a mix breed that is now known as a mini pig.

Around the same time, scientists also developed a mini pig called Minnesota Mini Pig which is a combination of feral boars, the Piney Rooter of Louisiana and black Guinean hogs. The Guam origins of a pig called Ras-n-Lama were also selected for the miniature pig experiment because of its Island dwarfism traits.

Today there are about 14 mini pig breeds and counting are being developed in U.S. labs to create a wider range of miniature pig varieties and color patterns. Mini pigs as house pets are increasingly gaining attention and will most likely continue to do so because it's unconventional but also unique.

Quick Facts

Pedigree: developed from feral wild hogs and Asiatic breeds; mixture of pig breeds across the world

Breed Size: small and compact

Length: not more than 15 inches (38 cm)

Weight: weighing under 55 pounds

Coat Length: short thick coat with patterns

Coat Texture: fine, silky, smooth

Color: Black, White, Black & White, Cream, Blue, Silver, Apricot, Strawberry, Tangerine, Auburn, Honey, Ash, Stone, Toffee, Champagne, Maple, Praline, Caramel, Pecan, Chestnut, Cinnamon, Chocolate, Mahogany, Roan and Agouti

Patterns/Markings:

Feet Type: Hoofs

Temperament: docile, gentle, friendly, active

Strangers: may be aggressive around strangers if not properly socialized

Other Pigs: generally good with other mini pig breeds if properly trained and socialized

Other Pets: friendly with other pets but if not properly introduce may result to potential aggression

Training: can be trained

Exercise Needs: provide toys for mental and physical stimulation

Health Conditions: generally healthy but predisposed to common illnesses such as Dippity Pig Syndrome, UTI, Pig Fever and Intestine Parasitism

Lifespan: average 12 to 18 years

Chapter Two: Miniature Pig Requirements

Are you now thinking of getting a mini pig as a pet? Awesome! After knowing what they are, their characteristics, and how to deal with them, it's time to give you practical tips on what you need to know before buying one.

In this chapter, you will get a whole lot of information on its pros and cons, its average associated costs as well as the legal licensing you need so that you will be well on your way to becoming a legitimate miniature pig pet owner – should you decide to be one! Let's do this!

Legal Requirements

If you are planning to acquire a mini pig as your pet, there are certain restrictions and regulations that you need to be aware of. Legal requirements for mini pigs may vary in different countries, regions, and states.

Here are some things you need to know regarding the acquirement of Miniature pigs both in United States and in United Kingdom.

United States Licensing for Mini Pigs

Before you bring home a new pet, it is always a good idea to determine whether there are any laws in your area which require you to register or license your pet.

In the United States, mini pigs are under the regulation of the USDA and several city governments. It is highly advisable that you check in first with your local government or ask authorities in your area about the rules before taking your mini pig home. There are certain zoning requirements that you may need to abide depending on which state or city you live. The reason for this is that many cities do not allow pigs as pets while in some cities there is a limit as to how many mini pigs you can keep.

It is highly recommended that you contact your city government offices to know the requirements but most likely it will fall under the cities livestock regulation.

Once you have read or learned about your city's zoning ordinance with regards to the mini pig restrictions or rules, you can apply or submit important documents or even file an official request regarding keeping your mini pigs as pets. Make sure that you also own a pet pig, preferably spayed or neutered already and is in great condition. You also want to make sure that these pigs are housed properly and are under your supervision when walking it outside.

Once you think you are prepared to make your case, you can then contact and set up a meeting with your city council or simply submit your proposal. Of course, the procedures and the offices that will handle your concern may vary from one city to another. Your proposal or request to keep your mini pig as a pet is not guaranteed.

United Kingdom Licensing for Mini Pigs

The licensing rules are quite different in United Kingdom and in many cases possibly much easier. The information below is applicable in England and Scotland only.

In the UK you need to register your mini pig first if you want to keep them. You can register as a pig keeper by getting a County Parish Holding (CPH) number from the RPA or the Rural Payments Agency. It is also imperative to tell the Animal and Plant Health Agency (APHA) that you are keeping pigs as pets within the span of at least 30 days after acquiring your mini pig. The Animal and Plant Health Agency will give you a herd mark which is a 1 or 2 letter with 4 digits, sort of like a code. This will serve as your mini pigs' identification whenever you travel with it or take it for a walk outside. However, before taking your mini pig for a walk you should first get a license at the APHA and give them your route. The agency may not approve your walking route it is passes near a livestock market, a fast food restaurant or a pig farm because it might pose a health risk.

You must also renew your license annually so that you can freely take your mini pig out for a walk.

Miniature Pigs and Other Pets

For the most part, mini pigs are developed and pretty much raised by humans so they usually enjoy being kept with other mini pigs. It is not necessarily a requirement that you keep two of the same kind of pig either as long as they are similar in size and their pen or your house provides ample space for both, you can keep different breeds of miniature pigs together. The best way to ensure harmony among your mini pigs is to raise them together from a young age while they are still babies, consult a vet or a mini pig breeder to know specifically the age in which they could be taken away from their mother mini pig.

Ideally one or two miniature pigs are fine; just make sure that before you get another one, you can provide for the needs of both pigs.

They may or may not get along that's for sure; there are many factors to consider like their individual temperament. Their tempers vary from one mini pig to another – some pigs might be very docile and unflappable while others may be a little more aggressive and wild. You also have to consider the temperament of your other pets such as your dog or cat. Some pets have a very low prey drive so you don't really have to worry about them chasing your mini pig around. Other breeds, however, particularly like hunting breeds, have a very high prey drive and if your mini pig has a high flight response because of its small size, it could lead to a dangerous chase.

When it comes to miniature pigs getting along with other household pets, the response is also highly varied. Younger miniature pigs may look more like prey to animals than adult or full grown mini pigs. If your pig is larger than you're your other pets, it probably won't be a problem but you still need to be careful. The best thing to do is to introduce your pets to each other while they are still young so they grow up together. Even then, you should still supervise their interactions to be safe.

Ease and Cost of Care

Owning a mini pig doesn't come cheap! The fact is that, these pigs require maintenance which means that you have to provide supplies and be able to cover the expenses in order to maintain a healthy lifestyle and environment for your pet.

These things will definitely add up to your daily budget, and the cost will vary depending on where you purchase it; the brand of the accessories, the nutrients included in its food and the time being. If you want to seriously own a mini pig as a pet you should be able to cover the necessary costs it entails.

In this section you will receive an overview of the expenses associated with purchasing and keeping a miniature pig such as food and treats, grooming and cleaning supplies, toys, and regular veterinary care. You will receive an overview of these costs as well as an estimate for each in the following pages of this section.

Initial Costs

The initial costs for keeping a mini pig include those costs that you must cover before you can bring your pig home. Some of the initial costs you will need to cover include your crate and play pen, food and water equipment, supplies and accessories, initial vaccinations, spay/neuter surgery and veterinary exams not to mention the cost of the mini pig itself. You will find an overview of each of these costs as well as an estimate for each below:

Purchase Price: $600 - $5,000

The cost to purchase a mini pig can vary greatly depending on the breed, where you buy him and whether it was pedigreed or not. You can probably find a backyard breeder offering $500 or below, but you cannot be sure of the breeding quality for these pigs. Generally speaking, pet-quality miniature pigs sell for $600 to as much as $5,000 maybe even more depending on the breeder as well.

Crate, Play Pen or Baby Gate: average of $100

Whether you live in a small apartment or have a large space in your backyard, you should definitely purchase a crate where your mini pig can stay and sleep in as well as a play pen or a baby gate to keep them safe and supervised as well as give them the freedom to move around. Crates and play pen have different sizes, on average it may cost about $100 but could vary depending on the brand and quality.

Food and Water Bowls: average of $30

In addition to providing your mini pigs with a cage or play pen, you should also make sure he has a set of high-quality food bowls and a water bowls. The best materials food bowls is stainless steel because it is easy to clean and doesn't harbor bacteria – ceramic is another good option. The average cost for a quality stainless steel bowl and a water bowl for pigs is about $30. Depending on the brand, some equipment could cost more than the average.

Initial Vaccinations: $50 and up

Mini pigs may require a couple of vaccinations especially during its young age. Your veterinarian can tell you if your mini pig needs any other vaccinations. To cover the cost of these vaccinations you should budget about $50 or more just to be prepared.

Spay/Neuter Surgery: $250 - $500

If you don't plan to breed your mini pig you should seriously consider having him or her neutered or spayed. Unfortunately, the cost to spay or neuter a pig breed is fairly high – around $250 to $500. However, if you keep two mini pigs of the same sex together, it may not be necessary, unless the rule in your city ordinance may require it.

Supplies/Accessories: average of $30

In addition to purchasing your mini pig's crate and other accessories, you should also purchase some basic grooming supplies like nail clippers for its hoof, bathing and cleaning supplies for its tusk and teeth as well as harness or a leash. You may also want to buy baby wipes for sanitary purposes. You might also want to consider buying a litter box if you want to litter train your rabbit. The cost for these items will vary depending on the quality and also quantity, so you should budget about $30 or more for these extra costs.

Veterinary Exams: average of $600 (annually)

In order to keep your mini pig healthy you should take him to the veterinarian at least every year. The average cost for an annual vet visit for a mini pig is about $600 or more not to mention other medical costs that may come up if your pet gets sick.

Needs	Costs
Purchase Price	$600 - $5000 (£490.19 - £4084.95)
Crate/Play Pen	$100 (£81.70)
Food/Water Equipment	$30 (£24.51)
Vaccinations	$50 (£40.85)
Spay/Neuter	$250 to $500 (£204.25 - £408.50)
Supplies/Accessories	$30 (£24.51)
Total	$1,060 to $5,710 (£866.01 – £4665.01)

*Costs may vary depending on location
**Costs may change based on the currency exchange

Monthly Costs

The monthly costs for keeping a mini pig as a pet include those costs which recur on a monthly basis. The most important monthly cost for keeping a mini pig is, of course, food. In addition to food, however, you'll also need to think about things like your bedding, litter, and veterinary exams. Here is the overview of each of these costs as well as an estimate for each need.

Food Pellet and Treats: $20 - $60

Feeding your mini pig a healthy diet is very important for his health and wellness. Later on in this book, you will learn how much your mini pig should eat and the kinds of food you can buy for him. Mini pigs feeds and treats needs to be replenish every month that's why you should budget about $20 - $60 per month for food; mini pigs also eat wheat and tasty treats depending on the your pig's appetite and size. You should also provide your pig with vegetables which can cost an extra $10 a month or so.

Bedding and Litter or Potty Pads: around $50 - $60

You may need to buy bedding for your mini pig as well as some blankets to keep them warm at night. Even if you don't use bedding in the whole cage, you should still provide some kind of hideaway lined with comfy bedding for your mini pig to sleep in.

It is also recommended that you replace your pigs' litter or potty pads once in a while. You should plan to spend about $50 - $60 a month on bedding and litter or potty pads for your mini pig.

Other Costs: around $15

In addition to the monthly costs for your pig's food, bedding, and litter, there are also some other cost you might have to pay occasionally. These costs might include things like cleaning or bathing products or repairs for the play pen. You should budget about $15 per month for extra costs just to be sure.

Needs	Costs
Food Pellet and Treats	$20 to $60 (£16.34 - £49.02)
Bedding/Litter	$50 - $60 (£40.85 - £49.02)
Other Costs	$15 (£12.25)
Total	$85 - $135 (£69.44 - £110.29)

*Costs may vary depending on location
**Costs may change based on the currency exchange

Pros and Cons of Miniature Pigs

Before you bring a mini pig home you should take the time to learn the pros and cons of the breed. Every mini pig breed is different so you need to think about the details to determine whether a mini pig is actually the right pet for you.

In this section you will find a list of pros and cons for mini pig breeds:

Pros for Miniature pigs

- Miniature pigs come in a variety of colors and patterns depending on the breed which allows you to choose the best option.
- They are intelligent yet emotional and sensitive
- They are active outdoors but can be controlled indoors
- They are hypoallergenic because instead of fur they have hairs.
- Miniature pigs are easily trained to use a litter pan - makes it easy to clean up after them.
- Generally a friendly, docile pet as long as there is proper introduction or socialization at a young age.
- Miniature pigs are easy to care for in terms of their diet – they eat mainly pellets, wheat, and fresh veggies.
- Miniature pigs do not require regular grooming and it can be done at home.
- Mini pigs are also trainable

Cons for Miniature pigs

- Mini pigs can be quite hard to register for licenses
- Mini pigs are cute but it can be a high maintenance pet especially in terms of needs

- Generally a good pet but some mini pig breeds may not be advisable for very small living spaces and may be restricted to places such as condos and apartments.
- They are prone to depression if left alone or for a long time by their owners
- May not be a good choice for a household that already has other pets, unless it is properly socialized.
- Generally not recommended for very young children who don't know how to handle or have never encountered a mini pig.
- Can be a long-term commitment – most rabbits live anywhere from 12 to 18 years or more.
- Cost for maintenance will definitely be additional expense.
- They are quite smelly and can also get messy around the house or backyard if not properly supervised
- They are highly motivated by food and can snoop around your kitchen, refrigerators, cabinets or trash cans – get ready for one wild hog chaos!

Chapter Three: Tips in Buying Miniature Pigs

Now that you are already aware and have prior knowledge about the legal aspects of owning and maintaining a mini pig as well as its pros and cons, the next step is purchasing one through a local farm pet store or a legitimate breeder. In this chapter you will find valuable information about where to find a mini pig breeder, how to select a reputable breeder, and how to choose a healthy mini pig from a litter. You will also receive tips for your home and for introducing your new pet pig to your family.

Choosing a Reputable Mini Pig Breeder

To make sure that you get a well-bred, healthy and robust piglet of your chosen breed, your best bet is to look around for a local breeder. You can feel free to ask around at your local pet store and you may also be able to get a personal recommendation from friends or your local veterinarian. Once you have your list of breeders on hand you can go through them one-by-one to narrow down your options.

Here are the following guidelines for you to be able to choose a reputable mini pig breeder:

Do a Background Check on the Breeder

Visit the website for each breeder on your list (if they have one) and look for key information about the breeder's history and experience.

- Check for licenses or document registrations to ensure the legitimacy of the breeder, if applicable.
- If the website doesn't provide any information about the facilities or the breeder you are best just moving on.

Interview the Breeders

Now that you have narrowed down some breeders, contact the remaining breeders on your list by phone

- Ask the breeder questions about his experience with breeding pigs in general and about the specific mini pig breed you are looking for.
- Ask for information about the breeding stock including registration or identification numbers and health information.
- Expect a reputable breeder to ask you questions about yourself as well – a responsible breeder wants to make sure that his pigs go to good homes.

Do an Onsite Inspection

Schedule an appointment to visit the facilities for the remaining breeders on your list after you've weeded a few of them out.

- Ask for a tour of the facilities, including the place where the breeding stock is kept as well as the facilities housing the mini pigs.
- If things look unorganized or unclean, do not purchase from the breeder.

- Make sure the breeding stock is in good condition and that the mini pigs are all healthy-looking and active.

Characteristics of a Reputable Breeder

By this time you should have narrowed down the best of the best breeders on your list, before making a decision consider every factor to make the most out of it. Make sure the breeder provides some kind of health guarantee and ask about any vaccinations the mini pigs may already have. Below are some characteristics you should look out for when selecting a reputable breeder.

- The breeder should be willing to educate or explain and answer all your questions expertly
- The breeder should allow on - site visits, however if you are far from the place, you should be able to request photos or videos from the breeder and he/she should gladly show them to you so that you won't waste your time.
- The breeder should offer a contract and some sort of warranty
- The breeder should be willing to take back or rehome the pig regardless of the situation

- The breeder should allow to be contact before and after purchasing the mini pig

- The breeder should be able to provide health records and also have contacts with veterinarian as well as firsthand information about the pigs' overall health
- The breeder should also explain to you the risks or the cons of keeping one as a pet not just the cons
- The breeder should be transparent and honest about how they raised and bred their stock so that you'll know that they're reputable and a caring owner as well.

List of Breeders and Rescue Websites

There are so many mini pig breeds to choose from, that's why you need to do some research and decide which breed you want before you start shopping around. When you are ready to buy a mini pig, you then need to start thinking about where you are going to get it. You may be able to find a mini pig at some local breeders near your area, but think carefully before you buy whether that is really the best option. Follow the quick guidelines mentioned earlier to ensure the quality of its breeding.

If you want a piglet or a baby mini pig, you can probably find some at rescue websites, you may also try adopting a mini pig from a reputable breeder as well, who knows it might be the better option for you. There are plenty of mini pigs out there who have been abandoned by their previous owners and they are looking for a new forever home. When you adopt a pig you are actually saving a life and there are some benefits for you as well!

Adopting a mini pig can sometimes be cheaper than buying from a breeder. Many mini pigs are ready for adoption and usually they have also already been spayed or neutered, litter trained, and could also be caught up on vaccinations.

Here is the list of breeders and adoption rescue websites around United States and United Kingdom:

United States Breeders and Rescue Websites

American Mini Pig Association
<http://americanminipigassociation.com/owners/find-breeder/>

Pixie Pigs
<http://www.pixiepigs.com/main_page.html>

Texas Tiny Pigs

<http://www.texastinypigs.com/>

When Pigs Fly Naked

<http://www.whenpigsflynaked.com/pigs-for-sale.html>

Charming Mini Pigs

<http://charmingminipigs.com/adoption-process/>

Sandy Creek Mini Pigs

<http://www.sandycreekminipigs.com/>

Juliana Pig Association

<http://www.julianapig.com/BreederDirectory.html>

Piggly Wiggly Mini Pigs

<http://www.pigglywigglyminipigs.com/

Teacup Pigs

<http://www.teacuppigs.info/>

Mini Pig Ranch

<http://www.minipigranch.com/shop>

Teacup Mini Pigs

<http://www.teacupminipigs.com/>

Teacup Piggies

<http://www.teacuppiggies.com/>

United Kingdom Breeders and Rescue Websites

Penny Well Farm

<https://www.pennywellfarm.co.uk/pigsaspets>

Pet Piggies UK

<http://www.petpiggies.co.uk/>

Courtney's Pet Pigs

<http://www.courtneyspetpigs.co.uk/>

Kew Little Pigs

<http://kewlittlepigs.com/>

Valley of the Pigs UK

<http://www.valleyofthepigs.co.uk/>

Micro – Pigs UK

<http://www.micro-pigs.net/>

Lancashire Micro Pigs UK

<http://lancashiremicropigs.co.uk/>

RSPCA Organization

<https://www.rspca.org.uk/adviceandwelfare/farm/farmani
mals/pigs>

Selecting a Healthy Mini Pig

After you have narrowed down your list of options to just two or three mini pig breeders, your next step is to actually pick out the piglet or mini pig you want. You have already determined that the remaining breeders on your list are responsible, but now you need to make sure that the mini pig they have available are healthy and ready to go home with their new owners.

Here are some few guidelines to keep in mind when selecting a healthy mini pig:

- **Check the Environment of the Mini Pigs**

Ask the breeder to give you a tour of the facilities. Make sure the facilities where the mini pigs are housed is clean and sanitary – if there is evidence of disease, do not purchase one of the mini pigs because they may already be sick.

- **Observe the Mini Pigs' Behaviors**

Take a few minutes to observe the stock as a whole, watching how the pigs interact with each other. Mini pigs should be active and playful, interacting with each other in a healthy way. Avoid any pigs that

appear to be lethargic and those that have difficulty moving – they could be sick.

- **Interact with the Mini Pigs**

  Put your hand inside the play pen or roam around with them inside it and give the mini pigs time to sniff and explore you before you interact with them. Pet the mini pigs and encourage them to play with you, taking the opportunity to observe their personalities. Then you can single out any of the mini pigs that you think might be a good fit and spend a little more time with them.

  You can also pick up the mini pigs and hold him to see how he responds to human contact. The mini pigs might squirm a little but it shouldn't be frightened of you and it should enjoy being pet.

- **Examine the Mini Pigs Body**

  Examine the mini pigs' body for signs of any illness and potential injury.

  Eyes: The mini pigs should have clear, bright eyes with no discharge.

Ears: Their ears should be clean and clear with no discharge or inflammation.

Body: The mini pigs body should be rounded without protruding bones.

Mobility: The mini pigs should be able to walk and run normally without any mobility problems.

Chapter Four: Caring for Your Miniature Pigs

The miniature pig makes a wonderful pet largely because of his energetic yet docile personality, but these pigs may or may not be adaptable to different types of living situations. In this chapter you will learn the basics about your mini pigs habitat requirements including the recommended cage type, useful accessories, and exercise requirements. You will also receive other general tips for training and handling your mini pig.

Habitat Requirements for Miniature Pigs

Unlike other pets, mini pigs need a space to roam around with. They are quite high maintenance because of their size especially when they became adults, even if they are considered as mini. But aside from space, the main thing your pet pig needs in terms of its habitat is lots of love and affection from his human companions and adequate exercise. Mini pigs are intelligent and cool breed that bonds closely with family, so you should make an effort to spend some quality time with your mini pig each and every day. If your pet doesn't get enough attention he may be more likely to develop behavioral problems, suffer from depression which can lead to potential aggression as well as separation anxiety.

In addition to playing with your mini pig and spending time with him every day, you also need to make sure that his needs for exercise are met. Mini pigs or pigs in general are the fifth most intelligent animal in the world that's why it's important for you to also make sure your pet gets plenty of mental stimulation during the day.

Keep reading to learn the basics about your pig's habitat requirements. You will also learn about recommended crate or kennel accessories and receive tips for choosing the right bedding for your pig as well as some guidelines on how to handle and train your pet.

Ideal Habitat for Mini Pigs

You can either put your mini pig in a kennel crate or set up a play pen around your house or backyard. Follow the guidelines below to ensure that your pet is comfortable.

- **Crate or Kennel**

Pig's natural instinct is to play or root in the mud and holes because that's where they get their nutrients and vitamins. Do not discourage them to do so. However, for the purpose of cleanliness around your house, you should also regulate the amount of mud they would jump in, you don't want dirt around your house all the time right? You can provide your pigs a play to stay in without compromising their natural habitat needs.

You can buy a 700 Series Veri Kennel that is preferably large or at least twice the size of your pigs. But it may cost you a couple of bucks. As an alternative you can build a three-sided shed yourself using a few ply woods. It's important to note that you should place the kennel where there are no prevailing winds and draughts. Pigs can only tolerate a temperature between 12 – 26 degrees Celsius otherwise it could be too hot or too cold for their body, this is why blankets are also needed during cold temperatures and a mud hole that they could splash in during hotter days because they don't sweat so they need to cool off. With that being said, your crate or kennel should at least have 8 square feet of space with rough unfinished flooring – it's good for their hoofs. It is also recommended for you to have a cemented space for them to get some exercise or sun bathe if they need to plus it could prevent smelly conditions as well.

Do not completely cement everything or let them sleep in a concrete flooring all the time, it is not good for their bones; their bodies thrive on the ground. Another important note you need to remember is to make sure that you provide enough shade or roofing for your pig so that they won't get sunburned or dehydrated.

- **'Play Space' or Pen Space**

If you don't want to let your pigs run loose in the house – and they will! You should provide a pen space in addition to your kennel. As mentioned earlier, pigs love to move freely and roam around; you should not restrict that because that is a form of exercise for them. A pigpen should be secured using a fence, preferably buy a breeze block wall around the shed that will serve as a pig-proof gate. You can also use wire-fence but it is expensive but is usually ineffective. Make sure that your fence is tight; pigs can spot a weakness and could use that opening to get out of his shed or kennel.

Recommended Kennel Accessories

In addition to providing your rabbit with a kennel and pen space, you also need to stock it with certain accessories. Here are a few things your pig needs for its habitat:

- **Water Bowl**

When it comes to your pig's water bowls, the larger the better and a flat surface is preferred to prevent it from tipping off. Provide as much water as possible because pigs need to be hydrated at all times, they don't have sweat glands so aside from stumping themselves into the mud, they need lots of water to cool off.

- **Food Bowl**

Food dishes for pigs come in all shapes and sizes but you should choose a set that suits your pet's needs. Miniature pigs are relatively small breeds, so don't choose anything too large. As mentioned in the previous chapters, stainless steel and ceramic bowls do not harbor bacteria like plastic can and they are easy to clean.

- **Hay Rack**

It is recommended that you buy a hay rack where you can place hays for your pig. Pigs love to nest and root in hay because it's a natural instinct.

- **Litter Pan**

Your pig's litter pan does not need to be anything fancy – it just needs to be large enough for your pig to turn around in and deep enough to contain the litter without making it hard for your pig to get into the pan. Make sure that you train your pig in identifying which is the litter pan and the water bowl; you need to constantly replace the contents of the bowls.

- **Bedding**

Your pig also needs a hiding place or shelter and of course a bedding. You may need to consider the type of litter you want to use for your pig's bedding – if you choose to use any at all. The best litter to use as mentioned earlier is fresh hay – ideally edible hay like meadow hay or timothy hay. You can also use a straw or blanket made from some kind of natural fiber. If you're living in an apartment and your kennel is in a concrete floor, then make sure to place a rubber mat so that you can hosed off the dirt but it's very important to put a lot of bedding sheets for your pig because as mentioned earlier, sleeping in on concrete floors are not suitable for them.

Potty Training for Mini Pigs

Mini pigs especially the young piglets do not have full bladder control, so if you don't want any litter around your house, you have to train them while they're young.

When it comes to potty training you have three options; you can use a litter pan inside, train them to poop outside or both. Usually it's better to do both. Changes in the weather may not permit your pig to defecate outside that's why you should train them using a litter pan inside the house. Young pigs need to start off with small litter boxes or pan until they are old enough to litter outside. Pigs do not want to soil their shed so it's better to put the litter box in a corner far away from where they sleep or eat but near enough so that they can easily find and remember it.

Here are some tips on how to potty train your pig inside the house:

- Put them in their potty box as often as possible, ideally after they eat and drink. Use reinforcement training and say "Go potty," they're intelligent creatures so if you make potty training in a litter a habit they will surely retain it.
- Make sure the litter pan is low enough so that your pig can easily enter.
- Do not change the potty spot as much as possible; make it a permanent litter spot for your pig. Once they learned where the spot is, they will always go there to poop because they have already developed it as a habit.
- Be prepared for "potty accidents" on the carpet or flooring.
- Make sure your mini pig mastered their potty training before you let them roam around your house.

Here are some tips on how to potty train your pig outside the house:

- Put up a confined or small area where they can poop
- After eating or drinking, take them outside in their designated potty area

- Use positive reinforcement, say phrases such as "good girl/boy" as well as commands such as "go poop"
- It's better to give them treats after they have successfully poop outside
- It will also help if you consistently take them outside when pooping for the first few weeks until they have mastered going on their potty spot by themselves.

Socializing and Training Your Mini Pig

At some point in time, you and your pet will already get along and are comfortable in each other, strengthen your relationship by taming them through training. Training a mini pig is not that hard to do, in fact it can be a fun and rewarding bonding experience for both of you.

There are lots of pet owners out there who have properly trained and raised a well-behaved mini pig. They are intelligent creatures that are highly motivated by food and routines. Trust is the most important key in training your mini pig. The first thing you need to do is to be able to establish a solid connection and rapport between you and your pet. This section will provide some guidelines you can do to get your mini pig well-behaved and disciplined. Are you ready? Read on!

Mini pigs make wonderful pets for a number of reasons but one of those reasons is that they are easy to train. The more time you spend with your pig, the more quickly he will get used to you and he will come to enjoy interacting with you.

If you are a new pig owner, it may take some practice to teach them some basic skills. One thing you can do is use small treats such as non-buttered and non-salted popcorn, wheat, cheerios, or small chunks of fruits to entice your mini pig to come to you and follow your command. Aside from using treats, you should also set specific time during the day for your training because pigs also liked routines. It is advisable to train them before bed time so that they will have a good night sleep. Physical exercises and mental workout is best done when your pig is focused, so don't do it right after eating their meal or when they are hungry.

Chapter Five: Meeting Your Miniature Pigs' Nutritional Needs

Feeding your mini pig is not that complicated. However, its breed types should be taken into consideration to meet its nutritional diet. Mini pigs, like many other pets, should be given the right amount of recommended food for a balanced nutrition because proper diet can lengthen the life expectancy of your mini pig.

In this section, you'll learn the majority of your pet's nutritional needs as well as feeding tips and foods that are good and harmful.

The Nutritional Needs of Mini Pigs

The entirety of a pigs' diet should be made up of
plant products as well as the right amount of pellet foods. It
is also important to realize that pigs love to eat a lot, as an
owner you should make sure that your pigs' nutritional
needs are met. It is actually quite simple – a balanced diet for
pigs should be made up of high-quality commercial
pellets/feeds, hays, fruits, and fresh vegetables. Your pigs
also need constant access to fresh water because this too
plays a role in your pigs' digestion. Below are the kinds of
food you should feed your pig.

- **Commercial Pellets**

When choosing high-quality commercial pellet/feeds to
use as your pig's staple diet, it is highly recommended that
you buy something from known reputable brands such as
Purina or Mazuri. If you want to know the specific grams or
cups to feed for your mini pig, it is better to consult your vet
or ask the breeder from whom you purchase the pig so that
there would be consistency on the kind of food your mini
pig eats. The amount of food highly depends on the weight
and breeding of your mini pig, which we will discuss later.

- **Grass Hays/ Grains**

Aside from choosing a quality pellet for your mini pig you should also stock up on fresh grass hay and wheat grains. Grass hay is loaded with calcium, vitamin A, vitamin D and other nutrients plus, the process of eating hay helps to keep your pig's digestive tract healthy and also makes you pig comfortable. Like the pellets, you want to make sure that your hay stays fresh.

- **Fresh Fruits**

In addition to fresh hays, you can also feed your rabbit small amounts of fresh fruit. It is also best to consult your vet on the amount of fruit you can give to your mini pig. Usually fruits only serve as treats for your pig. Below are the lists of fruits that are safe for miniature pigs:

- Apples (no seeds)
- Bananas
- Melon
- Blackberries
- Blueberries
- Boysenberries
- Breadfruit
- Gooseberries
- Canteloupe

- Coconut
- Cranberries
- Durian
- Figs
- Grapefruit
- Honeydew Melon
- Jackfruit
- Lemons
- Lychee
- Mango
- Orange
- Papaya
- Pear
- Passion fruit
- Pineapple
- Plums
- Strawberry
- Star Fruit
- Peach (no pits)
- Apricot (no pits)
- Cherry (no pits)
- Tangerines
- Watermelon
- Nectarines (no pits)
- Cherries

- **Fresh Vegetables**

Last but definitely not the least is fresh vegetables. Just like fruits, fresh veggies also serve as treats during training and use as positive reinforcement. Although commercial pellets comprise most of their diet, vegetables should still be included in your mini pigs' daily diet.

Here is a list of leafy green vegetables that are also safe for mini pigs:

- Acorn Squash
- Artichoke
- Asparagus
- Banana Squash
- Bamboo shoots
- Beets
- Bell Peppers
- Black olives
- Black Radish
- Broccoli
- Cabbage
- Carrots
- Cauliflower
- Celery Root

- Celery
- Cherry Tomatoes
- Chives
- Corn
- Cucumbers
- Dandelion
- Eggplant
- Galangal Root
- Green Beans
- Green leaf lettuce
- Edamame
- Lettuce
- Lettuce
- Mushrooms

- Mustard Greens
- Okra
- Olives
- Parsnips
- Peanuts (unsalted)
- Rhubarb stem/stalk
- Snow Peas
- Spinach
- Spring Baby Lettuce
- Sugar Snap Peas
- Sweet Potatoes

- Swiss chard
- Tomatoes
- Turnip greens
- Turnips
- Wasabi Root
- Watercress
- Winged Beans
- Winter Squash
- Yellow Squash
- Yucca Root
- Zucchini

Toxic Foods to Avoid

It might be tempting to give in to your mini pig when he is at the table, but certain "people foods" can actually be toxic for your pet. As a general rule, you should never feed your mini pig anything unless you are 100% sure that it is safe.

In this section you will find a list of foods that can be toxic to mini pigs and should therefore be avoided.

- Salt

- Plum – Leaves & seeds
- Broccoli – Roots & seeds
- Cabbage – Roots & seeds
- Mustard – Roots & seeds
- Lychee – seeds
- Rambutan – raw seeds
- Longan – seeds
- Taro – raw
- Cassava roots and leaves
- Almond – Leaves & seeds
- Acorns & oak leaves
- Moldy walnut shells
- Elderberries, red berries
- Lima beans, raw
- Nectarine – Leaves & seeds
- Cherry – Leaves & seeds
- Tomato leaves and vine
- Avocado – Skin and pit
- Corn stalks (high in nitrates)
- Rhubarb – Leaves (stalk is safe to eat)
- Kidney beans, raw
- Decayed sweet potatoes (black parts)

- Castor beans
- Potato leaves and green parts of potato
- Apple – Leaves & seeds
- Apricot – Leaves & seeds
- Pear – Leaves & seeds
- Peach – Leaves & seeds
- Tobacco – leaves
- Nutmeg- in large quantities

Healthy Treats

Every time your pet pig follows your command or did something good, you should reward him or her some healthy treats and snacks, this is also part of positive reinforcement. Here are some snacks you can feed your mini pig.

- Fruit Chips – Bananas, Apples
- Coconut Oil
- Coconut Water
- Cottage Cheese
- Yogurt, Plain or Greek
- 100% Pumpkin Canned
- Fruit Juice with no sugar added

- Gerber Toddler Puffs
- Applesauce, no sugar added
- Baby Food with no sugar or salt added
- Baked cookies or muffins
- Popcorn Air Popped
- Scrambled or hardboiled eggs
- Warmed/cooked oatmeal
- Whole eggs raw
- Whole Pumpkin
- Granola
- Peanut Butter on celery

Tips for Feeding Miniature pigs

Now that you know what to feed your mini pig you may be wondering what amount or how much to feed him. To make sure that your mini pigs gets the nutrients he needs; you need to adjust his diet based on his weight. Veterinarians and researchers agreed that mini pigs' proper diet should be 2% of its overall body weight. According to other sources it can go as low as 1% and as much as 3% for mini pigs who are parenting.

Obesity is the leading health problem for pigs in general because they love to eat. Do not over feed them or underfeed them as well because it will both result to your mini pigs craving for more.

Below are some tips on how to properly calculate your mini pig's diet based on the average 2% body weight rule.

- Determine your pig's weight or what your mini pig should weigh. Consult your vet or do your own research on the current weight of your pet and the ideal weight for the mini pig breed.
- Ideally and on average, your mini pig should eat 2% of its ideal weight per day. It is recommended that you scale the food and measure it properly.

Chapter Six: Breeding Your Miniature Pigs

Nothing is more adorable than a little baby mini pig – except for maybe a whole litter of them! If you decided to buy two mini pigs, for instance a male and female and keep them together, you should definitely prepare for the possibility of breeding, unless it's the same gender, otherwise you're going to be caught off guard! If you are interested in breeding your mini pigs, this chapter will give you a wealth of information about the processes and phases of its breeding and you will also learn how to properly raise mini pig on your own.

This not for everyone but if you want to have better understanding about how to raise these mini pig, then you should definitely not miss this part! On the contrary if you are interested in becoming a reputable breeder, then this is a must read chapter for you.

Basic Mini Pig Breeding Information

Before you can breed your mini pigs, you need to understand the basics of mini pig breeding. Most mini pigs are mature enough to be mated by the time they reach 4 to 7 months old. Keep in mind that the sexual maturity of mini pigs varies depending on the kind of breed. Male mini pigs are sexually mature at around 4 – 7 ½ months old but some male mini pig breeds may be sexually mature as early as 2 months old. Female miniature pigs are sexually matured and ready for breeding at about 6 – 7 months old. You can always ask your veterinarian if you aren't sure about your specific mini pig breed.

Unlike other animals, there is no average litter size for mini pigs or pigs in general. It can range from 1 to 12 piglets or more.

Signs that your Mini Pig is Pregnant:

Usually you won't be able to tell immediately whether your mini pig or the sow (mother pig) is pregnant unless your veterinarian have done some blood work or if your mini pig undergo through ultrasound. This is where most owners gets caught up; sometimes the pigs' belly just naturally appears to be bulky or fatty especially for obese pigs, so you may not notice it until you see some early pregnancy signs.

Within the succeeding weeks, your vet will be able to tell you how many piglets the sow is expecting. It is highly recommended that your mini pig regularly do a pregnancy check-up so that if ever any problem arises, your vet may be able to assist you because he/she knows your pig's history.

There are behavioral and physical signs to determine if your mini pig is pregnant. Here are some early signs you need to watch out for:

- The sow may have random mood swings and may become aggressive with other animals for no reason.
- She starts building a nest and will likely want to stay there most of the time.
- The sow also doesn't want to be disturbed and will not want other animals bother her – even you, be careful because some pigs that are pregnant tend to bite if they are disturbed.
- She may become restless or would want to chew anything and even try to escape the pen.
- Its mammary glands gradually enlarges and becomes firm; it will also secrete a clear fluid
- The vulvar lips will start to swell

Labor Process of Miniature Pigs

You will know if your mini pig is about to give birth if she started lying on her side. Don't approach her on the head but you can at least soothe her and put on a calming music because according to research it calms them. The gestation period is around 3 – 4 months.

About four days before farrowing or giving birth, the sows' vulva will start to swell, in the next 2 days the breast glands will become tense and will secrete a clear fluid. Within 24 hours, the sow will start to secrete milk, she will be more restless than ever and its respiration rate will increase. Usually when the sows' mood swings decreases, and if she started to quietly lay on her side, that's a sign that she will give birth in about an hour.

The sow will then lift her legs up to her belly and its tail will rapidly twitch, after which the straining will begin. You will see a tinged of blood coming out of its vulva; you can expect the first newborn piglet to come out within the next 15 – 20 minutes. The succeeding newborn piglets will have a 15 minute interval but for some breeds it could take longer. Labor duration usually lasts for as short as 30 minutes to as long as 5 hours or more. The placenta is excreted 2 – 4 hours after the last pig was born but portion of it may come out during farrowing. If the interval time of the pigs exceeds an hour intervention is necessary.

Important Note

If your mini pig gave birth for first time they may tend to have a temporary weird and aggressive temperament. It may cause them to kill or bite their piglets, which is why you need to remove the piglets away from their mother for a while and slowly put them near her after a few minutes and see how she reacts. Once the sow is tamed, you can lead the other piglets to her for breast feeding.

Caring for Newborn Piglets

Once your mini pig gives birth, you need to provide more hays than ever. It will serve as nest for the newborn piglets and a couple of blankets or drying agents to keep them warm. Newborn piglets tend to lose heat very quickly; usually their average temperature is around 100 – 105 degrees Fahrenheit. They should be dry immediately for about 5 minutes after coming out and they should be free from drafts. It is highly recommended that you put a heater or light over the newborns; the temperature should be about 80 to 90 degrees and keep it for at least 8 to 10 days. Piglets cannot produce body heat on their own yet so it's important to keep them warm.

If you want your piglet to survive and also become healthy in the long run, newborns should be given access to their mother's milk. The colostrum or first milk is needed because it is enriched with immunoglobulin. Allow the mini pigs to nurse their offspring for about 5 hours or more.

Some piglets may be abnormal or disabled, usually these piglets are lightweight than the average, they are

chilling or may have splayed legs, some are even anemic –
you can identify the anemic pigs by their grayish color.
These piglets should be assisted when nursing and when
they are drinking milk from their mothers. It is highly
recommended that you consult a veterinarian to know the
specific procedures for different mini pig breeds that are
disadvantaged.

Chapter Seven: Grooming Your Miniature Pigs

Different mini pig breeds may have different coat conditions and textures so take the time to explore your pig's coat in order to determine what his grooming needs might be. Grooming your mini pig helps to distribute its natural body oils to keep his skin healthy, shiny, and soft. No matter what kind of coat your mini pig has, it is your job to groom it properly so it remains in good health. In this chapter you will learn the basics about grooming your mini pig – this includes brushing and bathing your pig as well as trimming his hoofs or nails, cleaning his tusk, and brushing his teeth.

Recommended Tools for Grooming

In order to keep your pig's coat clean and in good condition you will need to have a few grooming tools on hand. Since pigs have a short coat and are hypoallergenic (they don't have fur, just hairs) you don't need to buy a brush. Here are some of the grooming tools that may come in handy when it comes to grooming and bathing your mini pig:

- Soap
- Shampoo
- Lotion
- Hard wire cutter
- Large nail cutter
- Metal File
- Rasp
- Toothbrush
- Baking Soda/Toothpaste
- Baby Wipes

Learning how to groom your mini pigs effectively is a task that takes time to learn. If you have no idea where to start or how to do it, it wouldn't be a bad idea to talk to a fellow mini pig owner or take your mini pig to a professional groomer so they can show you what to do, you can also consult your vet for some tips. On the next section, you will be provided with an overview on how easily clean your pig.

Tips for Bathing and Grooming Miniature Pigs

Unlike other pets or animals, mini pigs and pigs in general love to splash in the water and take a bath! They will surely enjoy it and for sure you will too.

Some owners bathe their mini pigs once or twice a day. Ideally, you want to do it in the morning after they eat breakfast or midday (after playtime) and after dinner so that they won't be covered in food or dirt before bedtime. You can also clean their noses using baby wipes. Pigs don't need to have a long bath; it could only take about 10 – 15 minutes and the water should be lukewarm.

There are no restrictions when it comes to the kind of soap, shampoo and even lotion you can use. Whatever works for human are also often times applicable for your pig pet. However, before applying any soap or shampoo make sure to check the chemical content first, it is also wise to ask your vet on the kinds of bathing products that is good for your pig. When bathing be extra careful to not let the soap or shampoo get into their eyes. You can also use a germ oil to keep mites away from your pig and keep its coat healthy and soft.

Bathe your pig regularly; you can also bathe them in your bathtub (make sure to provide a rubber mat so that your mini pig won't slip). Keep in mind that a cooling bath or playtime in the bathtub helps in bringing down your pig's body temperature because they can't sweat on their own. After bathing, you can now damp a soft towel or cloth to dry them off, usually they will scream at you if you mess with their bathing time, but it's normal. Just wait for them to calm down and sit them right up so you can rinse them off.

Grooming sessions is a great way for you to bond with your pig so make it fun for you and your pet!

Other Grooming Tasks

In addition to bathing your mini pig on a regular basis, there are some other simple grooming tasks you should be prepared to perform fairly often. These include trimming your mini pig's hoofs, trimming his tusk, and taking care of its teeth.

Trimming Your Mini Pig's Hoofs

Hoof trimming should be done while they're still young so that they will get used to it. Before you cut or shape your mini pig's hoofs or nails, make sure to understand first the anatomy of its hoofs. It's important to know which are the hard tissue and the soft tissue; of course you would want to cut the excess nails or hard tissue and not the pig's flesh. You can use trimming tools such as a hard wire cutter, large nail cutter, or a metal file. The tools will likely change as your mini pig hooves grows thicker and harder.

To begin cutting your pig's nails, you may want to let your mini pigs lie on their side and check the hooves one at a time. You need to also remove the dirt on its hooves so you can clearly identify the hard tissue or the nails. Once you do, you can start trimming and shaping them but do it carefully and slowly you don't want to scare your mini pig. Cut it accordingly and in parallel to its heels and toes, after which you can use a rasp or dremel to smoothen the rough edges of its nails. You also need to cut the dew claws of your mini pig.

You can consult your vet on how to properly cut your mini pig's nails or bring him to a professional groomer.

Trimming Your Mini Pig's Tusk

Mini pigs like normal sized pigs have tusks, they can either be trimmed or not. It is ideal that you trim your pig's tusk depending on what kind of breed it is, how long it grows over time and the risk for people as well. Tusks may grow rapidly depending on the breed and often times it is sharp, that's why it could dangerous to people especially for owners with young children.

The schedule of tusk trimming is entirely up to you, some owners do it once a year; others are on a monthly basis while other people only do it when necessary. It's better to bring your mini pig to the vet if you want its tusk to be trimmed; you need an expert for this because if you try to do it yourself and hurt the pig they could suffer from trauma and experience a Porcine Stress Syndrome which is fatal. Once you bring your pet to the vet, you can also discuss anesthesia options to aid in the tusk trimming.

Caring for Your Mini Pig's Teeth

You can leave the brushing of your mini pig's teeth to a professional groomer or vet but in case you want to cut the expenses, you can do it yourself. You just need to provide a toothbrush (ideally a pet toothbrush but human toothbrushes are fine) and toothpaste that doesn't contain fluoride – fluoride can be poisonous to your pet; baking soda is preferred.

Just like in trimming your mini pig's tusk and hooves, it's better to start brushing their teeth while they are still young so that it will be easier for you when they're older because they'll be used to it. Piglets start to grow teeth when they are about one year old. You can carefully touch their teeth and put your fingers slowly until they are comfortable with it, then you can start brushing them, be careful though you don't want to hurt their gums. You can also use a washcloth for brushing.

Chapter Eight: Showing Your Miniature Pig

The mini pig is a wonderful pet to keep but this creature has the potential to be so much more than that. In order to show your mini pig, however, you have to make sure that he meets the requirements for the breed standard and you need to learn the basics about showing mini pigs.

In this chapter you will learn more about the specific standard for the mini pig and receive some tips for entering them in a show. This information will help you to decide if showing your mini pig is really something you want to do.

American Mini Pig Standard

Unlike normal sized pig breeds or hogs, mini pigs cannot participate in official contests such as hog shows or swine shows because it is developed solely as a pet companion and therefore cannot qualify for hog standards. However, you can still show off your mini pigs by participating in several costume or designer shows where owners get to dress up their pets. Although these shows mainly judge your mini pig's dress, sometimes they may also include the mini pig breed standard and the tricks it can do in the criteria for judging. Below is the standard size for an American Mini Pig.

Body Size and Condition

- Measures about 15 – 20 inches from the top of the shoulders at 5 years old.
- Overall weight may vary but it should be proportionate with its stature
- The mini pig should have no mobility issues and should be able to run and move freely with no support

Head

- The head of your mini pig should be proportionate to its body

- The eyes should not be obstructed; must be open and should have a clear vision; there should be no eye discharge
- The teeth and mouth should have no defect; it must be clean, proportional and free from dental or mouth diseases
- The forehead slopes to its snout length may vary but it should be proportional

Ears

- It should be erect
- Must be relatively small and proportional

Neck

- Must have no excessive jowls or should not have a fatty neck
- Must be proportionate to its body

Body

- The mini pig's body should be proportional, compact and well-balanced.
- Preferably has a strong and athletic appearance

Back

- The mini pig's back should be vertical or straight without a prominent sway

Tail

- Its tail should be natural and straight
- It should have a tassel at the end

Feet and Legs

- The legs should be proportionate, straight and must look strong and appealing
- The toes in its hooves should be even and facing forward

Hair

- The mini pig's hair should be healthy and coarse
- Its length and thickness should adapt with the season

Color

- The American mini pigs have a wide variety of colors and patterns (color/pattern requirements may vary from one contest to another)

Sexual Characteristics

- Males should have two proportional palpable testicles set in the scrotum
- Females mammary glands should at least have 12 inch space interval

Temperament

- Mini pigs should be friendly, has an even or calm temperament, intelligent and can do tricks

Disqualification

- If mini pig suffers from illnesses and abnormalities such as hernia, mule foot, heavy wrinkling, swayed back, wattles etc.

<u>Important Note</u>

Mini pigs breed and qualification standard may vary in one contest to another. The guidelines provided in this section are only based on the American Mini Pig Association. The mini pig standard can also be used as a guide when purchasing or choosing a mini pig from a breeding stock.

Preparing Your Mini Pig for Show

If you will be in an environment that has a lot of pigs and people, make sure that your mini pig can socialize well.

- It's important that you know the rules of the show, so that you and your mini pig can act accordingly. It's best that before entering any mini pig contests you have observed and/or attended previous shows or contests before as part of an audience so that you'll have an idea on how it works.

- Check the requirements and pig standards, so you could know if your mini pig meets all the requirements for registration
- Few weeks before the show, you must have trained your mini pigs to at least have some basic tricks to show off its abilities and discipline (although in costume contests this may not be necessary)
- The mini pig should learn how to listen and follow basic commands, solidify your pig's grasp of basic obedience and make it learn how to behave so that it won't cause disturbances with other mini pig participants.
- Have your vet clear his overall health for the show, make sure your mini pig's body condition is healthy
- Take the necessary steps to keep your pig's coat clean and in good condition. You can brush it with soft bristled brush and spray a mist of water to its hair
- Brush off dirt or sand with baby wipes or a soft towel before your mini pig is called for presentation
- Keep your mini pig under control; always keep treats in your pockets and walk him or her quietly but with finesse.

It is better for you to pack a bag of supplies that you will need on the day of the show, as you have already taken into account the requirements for the show and mini pig breed standard guidelines. This is a list for helpful things to put in your supply pack for your mini pig show:

- Information for registration
- Washing Supplies
- Brushes or other grooming tools
- Small whip (optional)
- Rags/Towels/Baby Wipes
- Treats and food
- Water and food bowls
- Trash bags for poop
- Medications (if the veterinarian prescribes it)
- Clothes for changing
- Food and water that you need

If you want to show your pig but you don't want to jump immediately into major competitions, you may be able to find some local mini pig shows in your area. Local shows may be put on by a branch of a mini pig breed club or associations and they can be a great place to learn and to connect with other owners.

Chapter Nine: Keeping Your Miniature Pig Healthy

You as the owner should be aware of the potential threats and diseases that could harm the wellness of your mini pig. Just like human beings, you need to have knowledge on these diseases so that you can prevent it from happening in the first place. You will find tons of information on the most common problems that may affect your rabbit including its causes, signs and symptoms, remedies and prevention. While you may not be able to prevent your rabbit from getting sick in certain situations, you can be responsible in educating yourself about the diseases that could affect your miniature pig.

The more you know about these potential health problems, the better you will be able to identify them and to seek immediate veterinary care when needed.

Common Health Problems Affecting Mini Pigs

Pet miniature pigs can be affected by a number of different health problems and they are generally not specific to any particular breed. Feeding your pig a nutritious diet will go a long way in securing his total health and wellbeing, but sometimes mini pigs get sick anyway. If you want to make sure that your pig gets the treatment he needs as quickly as possible you need to learn how to identify the symptoms of disease. These symptoms are not always obvious either; your mini pig may not show any outward signs of illness except for a subtle change in behavior.

The more time you spend with your pet pig, the more you will come to understand his behavior – this is the key to catching health problems early. At the first sign that something is wrong with your mini pig you should take inventory of his symptoms – both physical and behavioral – so you can relay them to your veterinarian who will then make a diagnosis and prescribe a course of treatment. The sooner you identify these symptoms, the sooner your vet can take action and the more likely your mini pig will be able to make a full recovery.

Mini pigs are prone to a wide variety of different diseases, though some are more common than others. For the benefit your mini pig's long-term health, take the time to learn the causes, symptoms, and treatment options for some of the most common health problems.

Below are some of the most common health problems that can occur to miniature pigs. You will learn some guidelines on how these diseases can be prevented and treated as well as its signs and symptoms.

Dippity Pig Syndrome

Dippity Pig Syndrome is also referred to as Erythema Multiforme or Bleeding Back Syndrome. This syndrome is an acute skin condition that is usually found along the backs of mini pigs and it is very common among piglets (around 4 months old). It can be very painful for your pet if not treated immediately.

Cause

Up until now, researchers and veterinarians cannot determine the cause of the dippity pig syndrome, however, some scientists say that this could somehow come from herpes virus and there are some evidences from biopsy tests that it is genetic and occurs in the pigs' lineage.

Signs and Symptoms

There are a lot of signs that your mini pig or piglets have dippity pig syndrome. If you notice your pet always screaming in pain, or having a temporary dipping of its hind legs and have sores on its back, it's a sure indicator that your pet is suffering from this illness. Others symptoms include showing red stripes along its back and a sudden onset in its attitude.

Prevention and Treatment

There is no actual treatment for this syndrome but the good thing is that the pain is only temporary and it only lasts for about 4 days max. However, you can do simple measures to help your pet become comfortable during this painful process. You can reduce the stress around him by providing comfortable bedding, soft music and also try to isolate them from other pets or even people so that they can rest. You can also give some medication such as a buffered aspirin or a Tylenol. Your vet could also give you something like Tramadol to reduce the pain, it's better to bring your pet to the vet so they can give the proper medication your mini pig needs.

Urinary Tract Infection

UTI is very common in pets and mini pigs are no exception. Of course, different pig breeds will show different symptoms and would also be given different treatment. If you think something is not right with your mini pig, it's safe to assume that he/she might have a UTI, just take a urine sample of it or bring it to the vet.

Cause

UTI can be caused by stress, heat cycle or hormonal changes, various infections, and bladder or kidney stones.

Signs and Symptoms

Clinical signs of UTI in mini pigs include frequent urination, fever, change in the color and odor of the urine, irritability, loss of appetite and lethargy.

Prevention and Treatment

If in case your mini pig has a UTI or if you think the symptoms is caused by UTI, you need to take your pig to your vet as soon as possible. It's would be better if you obtain a fresh urine sample of your pet and have your vet analyze it for infection or abnormalities. The usual treatment for UTI is antibiotics.

Pig Fever

Just like in humans, fever is an indicator that something is wrong in the body, in this case, your pig's body.

Cause

If your pet pig has a fever chances are he/she has a viral or bacterial infection, allergies, inflammation, or he ingested a toxin and could also be bitten by bugs or insects.

Signs and Symptoms

The most common sign of fever is of course the rise of its body temperature, just like in humans, it's the body's self-defense to wipe out the bacterial or viral infection, so if your mini pig's body temperature doesn't drop no matter what first aid medicines you give to him or her, that only means that it's not cause by an infection. Bring your pet immediately to the veterinarian.

Treatment

If your pig has a fever and you can't immediately bring it to your vet you can do a first aid treatment. You can increase its fluid intake; try offering fruit juices such as apple or cranberries and also a few meals. You can also give them ice cubes wrapped up in ice packs if in case he/she wants to cool itself. It's important that you don't give them a full bath at this time. Do not also give them any kind of aspirin but you may try offering them a Tylenol every 8 hours for at least 3 days. If symptoms persist more than 3 days consult your vet.

Abscesses

An abscess is a pocket of fluid and pus generally cause by a bacterial infection. These are fairly common in mini pigs as well as farm pigs in general because they can form anywhere on the pig's body.

Cause

The cause of an abscess could be any number of things including a bite, a cut, or some other kind of wound – they may also be caused by foreign bodies becoming embedded in the pigs' skin.

Signs and Symptoms

Abscess can be very painful for your mini pig and it may cause him to stop eating or loss appetite. He may also drool and drop bits of food when he does eat. Abscesses on the skin usually appear as hard lumps.

Prevention and Treatment

The best treatment for an abscess is to drain the fluid and pus which is usually performed under general anesthesia. Following the drainage, the wound must be kept clean and painkillers may also be prescribed, it's better to discuss options with your veterinarian.

Ringworms

Ringworms or intestinal worms are another common illness for pigs. You may not completely be aware of it so it's better for your mini pig especially piglets to undergo deworming process to prevent further illnesses.

Signs and Symptoms

If your mini pig has intestinal worm, there won't be any visible signs but you can always check their poop every now and then. If you see worms that looks like a pasta, that's a sign that you mini pig has a lot of ringworms. You won't notice physical symptoms until they have affected your pig's immune system.

Prevention and Treatment

To prevent the spread of ringworms or other intestinal parasites, you may want to deworm your pig as early as 6 weeks old. You can also do it twice a year or after every 6 months for prevention. You buy over the counter treatments such as Doramectin or Fenbendazole to deworm your pig, consult your vet for further specifications.

Pneumonia

Pneumonia is another common illness with pigs especially with young mini pigs. It is generally caused by some kind of infection – bacterial or viral in most cases – which leads to inflammation in the lungs.

Cause

Pneumonia can result from four different types of infections. It can either be bacterial, viral, fungal, or parasitic. It is also possible for environmental factors such as chemicals, smoke, or dental disease to cause inflammation which leads to pneumonia. Usually the climate conditions also affect piglets.

Signs and Symptoms

Pneumonia in animals have similar symptoms such as sneezing, nasal discharge, fever, anorexia, weight loss, eye discharge drooling and difficulty breathing.

Prevention and Treatment

The type of infection will determine the severity of the disease as well as the proper course of treatment. Piglets suffering from pneumonia could be fatal. Your vet may also prescribe antiviral, antimicrobial, antifungal, or antibiotic medications depending on the type of infection causing your pig's pneumonia.

Scabies

Scabies or otherwise known as Sarcoptic Mange are cause by external parasite known as mites. It is microscopic parasites that invade and infect the skin's pig. It is one of the most common problems with mini pigs and farm pigs as well.

Causes

The cause of scabies infestation is still unknown, but it is likely that some pigs carry the mites unknowingly and problems only develop when pigs are weakened by stress, illness, or injury. Mites feed on keratin which leads to poor coat condition and skin quality.

Signs and Symptoms

The most common sign of scabies in pigs are head and ear shaking, development of tiny pimple like allergies, and excessive scratching which leads to severe rubbing of the skin that could cause bleeding. It may take approximately three weeks before symptoms appear but sometimes it could take months before these signs are noticed.

Prevention and Treatment

Treatment for scabies generally involves Dectomax or Ivermectin injection or through mixing it with the pigs food. Consult your vet if symptoms persist. Regular grooming or bathing will also help prevent reinfection.

Preventing Illness

In addition to learning about the different diseases to which your mini pig may be prone, there are some other simple things you can do to keep your pet healthy. For one thing, you need to keep your pig's pen clean. Not only will cleaning your pig's playpen help to prevent the spread of parasites, bacteria, and other harmful pathogens but it will also help to keep your pig's stress level low – if you pig becomes stressed, it could compromise his immune system and he may be more likely to get sick if he is exposed to some kind of illness.

It is important to note that you should also be mindful of making sure that your pig gets the right vaccinations and you should take steps to protect your mini pig against parasites.

In this section you will find guidelines on how you can prevent unwanted illnesses that could endanger your pig's life.

- **Sanitize Your Mini Pig's Cage**

When it comes to cleaning your mini pig's cage, you may want to disinfect everything.

Start by emptying everything out of your pig's playpen or kennel – that includes bedding, food bowls, and blanket and, of course, your mini pig. After cleaning out your pig's kennel, disinfect it with a pig-friendly cleaner or just simply buy a safe spray which you can get in the grocery store. After cleaning and disinfecting your pig's kennel you need to do the same for his food and water equipment as well as other accessories. You may want to wash or scrub the beddings or accessories thoroughly using bleach or other cleaning products suitable for pigs or pets in general.

When you are done cleaning and disinfecting, add some fresh bedding to the pen and put everything back. As long as you keep to a regular schedule, you shouldn't have to clean your pigpen more than once a week, if you think it's necessary, over cleanliness wouldn't hurt.

- **Preventing Parasites**

Just like other pets, your mini pig needs protection against mites and other parasites. If one pig has a parasite or is infected with mites, it will most likely spread with other pigs or even pets near it. Consider protecting your pig with a topical flea control preventive, it is recommended that you ask your veterinarian for recommendations on which brand to use and follow the dosing instructions very carefully.

As mentioned earlier mites can cause scabies or flakey patches of irritation on your pig's skin. It is better to talk to your veterinarian if you notice any of these problems happening to your mini pig.

Recommended Vaccinations

Mini pigs need vaccinations especially while they are still young. These vaccinations will help prevent various illnesses and could also act as a booster for its immune system. Take your pet to the veterinarian to discuss the vaccination your pig needs. Below is the list of common and general vaccines that you should give to your pet.

Erysipelas Vaccine

Erysipelas is caused by birds that stays in the soil and therefore and pose a threat to your mini pig. Give your pig an erysipelas vaccine at about 8 weeks old, with a booster in 2 weeks. Then do it on a yearly basis.

Tetanus Vaccine

Tetanus is also a threat that is found in the soil, and can also cause infection or even fatality especially when contacted with a scratch or wound of your mini pig. Give your pig a tetanus vaccine, with a booster in 2 weeks. Then do it every 6 months.

Leptospirosis Vaccine

This is carried by infected urine of animals or pests such as rats and raccoons. It can infect your mini pig through water contamination. Give your pig a leptospirosis vaccine, with a booster in 2 weeks. Then do it on a yearly basis.

Actinobacillus Pleuropneumoiae Vaccine

This vaccine is given to boost your pig's immune system and it is included as a general vaccine for mini pigs especially for breeding pigs to protect their unborn piglets from various diseases.

Rabies Vaccine

Usually rabies vaccines for mini pigs are the same with what is being used for dogs. It is not mandatory or required for pigs because they don't really bite people. However you can still have the option to have them vaccinated. It should be done at 4 months of age, with a booster in 1 year. Then you can do it after every 3 years.

Signs of Possible Illnesses

- **Eating Disorders** – does your pig show signs of appetite loss or drooling and dropping of food?
- **Coat** - does its coat and skin still feel soft, firm and rejuvenated? If your pig is ill or infected, it appears physically on its body and can have a poor coat condition or hair loss.
- **Mobility** – does your pig looks like it is out of balance?
- **Eyes** - are there any discharge in the eyes? Is it swelling?
- **Ears** – does the ear of your pig swells or droops?

- **Respiratory** – does your pig have difficulty in breathing?
- **Nose** - does your pig have a watery nasal discharge?
- **Overall Physique** - does your pig stays active or are there any signs of weakness and deterioration?

First Aid Kit You Need In Case of Emergencies

Here are some things that may come in handy when treating minor illnesses for your mini pig or in case of emergencies. Make sure you have them in your home at all times.

- Oatmeal
- Canned Pumpkin
- Karo Syrup
- Low Sodium Chicken Broth
- Heating Pad
- Prilosec or Pepcid
- Pepto Bismol
- Ivermectin and Syringe for worming
- Syringes for Dosing Medications
- Ice Pack
- Gatorade or Pedialyte
- Digital Thermometer

- Poison Control Number
- Hydrogen Peroxide 3%
- Buffered Aspirin or Children's Tylenol
- Benedryl
- Emergency Vet Number

Miniature Pig Care Sheet

Congratulate yourself! You are now on your way to becoming a very well-informed and pro-active Miniature Pig owner! Finishing this book is a huge milestone for you and your future or present pet, but before this ultimate guide comes to a conclusion, keep in mind the most important things you have acquired through reading this book.

This chapter will outline the summary of what you have learned, including the checklist you need to keep in mind to ensure that you and your Miniature Pig lived happily ever after!

Basic Information

Pedigree: developed from feral wild hogs and Asiatic breeds; mixture of pig breeds across the world

Breed Size: small and compact

Length: not more than 15 inches (38 cm)

Weight: weighing under 55 pounds

Coat Length: short thick coat with patterns

Coat Texture: fine, silky, smooth

Color: Black, White, Black & White, Cream, Blue, Silver, Apricot, Strawberry, Tangerine, Auburn, Honey, Ash, Stone, Toffee, Champagne, Maple, Praline, Caramel, Pecan, Chestnut, Cinnamon, Chocolate, Mahogany, Roan and Agouti

Patterns/Markings:

Feet Type: Hoofs

Temperament: docile, gentle, friendly, active

Strangers: may be aggressive around strangers if not properly socialized

Other Pigs: generally good with other mini pig breeds if properly trained and socialized

Other Pets: friendly with other pets but if not properly introduce may result to potential aggression

Training: can be trained

Exercise Needs: provide toys for mental and physical stimulation

Health Conditions: generally healthy but predisposed to common illnesses such as Dippity Pig Syndrome, UTI, Pig Fever and Intestine Parasitism

Lifespan: average 12 to 18 years

Habitat Requirements

Ideal Habitat: free-run in the home or backyard with some kind of kennel or play pen with opportunities to exercise

Kennel Requirements: large enough for mini pig to move freely, easy to clean, and safe

Ideal Cage Size: 700 Series Veri Kennel; at least twice you mini pig's size

Exercise Requirements: at least every day and during training

Cage Accessories: water bottle, food bowl, beddings, litter pan or box, hay stack, blankets

Recommended Bedding: natural fiber blanket, straw, and pine

Litter Training: place litter pan or box in the area your mini pig habitually uses to relieve himself

Recommended Litter: fresh hay lined with newspaper

Nutritional Needs

Diet Type: herbivore

Nutrition Basics: rich in protein and fiber

Dietary Staples: high-quality commercial pellets, fresh hay, grains, fresh vegetables, fresh fruits, healthy snacks

Pellets: Purina or Mazuri; amount of food highly depends on the weight and breeding of your mini pig

Hay: timothy hay and other grass hays is a staple; supplement with oat hay

Vegetables: leafy greens should make up at least 70% of fresh diet

Fruit: should be within 2% of bodyweight daily just like vegetables but not too much, just a few pieces or slices a day will do

Water: unlimited access to fresh water at all times

Breeding Information

Sexual Maturity (female): average 4 to 7 ½ months old

Sexual Maturity (male): average 6 to 7 months old

Breeding Age (female): around 6 to 7 months

Breeding Age (male): around 6 to 7 months

Breeding Type: multiple cycles per year, continuous

Mating Protocol: add the --- to the sow's pen; rebreed at least one for better chance of success

Palpation: should be able to feel marble-sized embryos or see mini pig hooves after few weeks since mating

Litter Size: 1 to 12 piglets

Breeding Interval: about 15 minutes

Labor Duration: 30 minutes to 5 hours

Placenta Excretion: 2 – 4 hours (if placenta is not excreted after 4 hours, consult your veterinarian)

Piglet Temperature: 100 – 105 degrees Fahrenheit

Required Temperature for Newborns: 80 to 90 degrees; keep it for at least 8 to 10 days

Index

M

N

P

V

W

PHOTO CREDITS

Page 1 Photo By Alexas_Fotos via Pixabay.com, <https://pixabay.com/en/piglet-wildpark-poing-baby-1326946/>

Page 21 Photo By Alexas_Fotos via Pixabay.com, <https://pixabay.com/en/piglet-wildpark-poing-small-pigs-1313045/>

Page 34 Photo By Alexas_Fotos via Pixabay.com, <https://pixabay.com/en/piglet-wildpark-poing-baby-1326950/>

Page 49 Photo By Jon Osborne via Flickr.com, <https://www.flickr.com/photos/jonno101/6306952722/in/photolist>

Page 60 Photo By violetta via Pixabay.com, <https://pixabay.com/en/pig-animals-nature-creature-animal-301308/>

Photo 71 By Alexas_Fotos via Pixabay.com, <https://pixabay.com/en/piglet-wildpark-poing-baby-1326948/>

Page 81 Photo By Alexas_Fotos via Pixabay.com, <https://pixabay.com/en/piglet-mirroring-water-bank-1409289/>

Page 82 Photo By FraukeFeind via Pixabay.com,
<https://pixabay.com/en/piglet-pigs-mini-pigs-happy-pig-377764/>

Page 88 Photo By Saumotions via Flickr.com,
<https://www.flickr.com/photos/saumotions/20111502510/>

Page 95 Photo By Alexas_Fotos via Pixabay.com,
<https://pixabay.com/en/piglet-mirroring-water-bank-1409290/>

Page 102 Photo By Alexas_Fotos via Pixabay.com,
<https://pixabay.com/en/piglet-wildpark-poing-small-pigs-1313042/>

Page 119 Photo By Richard Elzey via Flickr.com,
<https://www.flickr.com/photos/elzey/20143829788/>

REFERENCES

"American Mini Pig Breed Standard" American Mini Pig Association
<http://americanminipigassociation.com/uncategorized/american-mini-pig-breed-standard/>

"Healthy Foods" American Mini Pig Association
<http://americanminipigassociation.com/mini-pig-education/mini-pig-nutrition/healthy-foods/>

"How to Pick a Breeder" American Mini Pig Association
<http://americanminipigassociation.com/mini-pig-education/how-to-pick-a-breeder/>

"Keeping a Pet Pig or Micropig" Gov.uk
<https://www.gov.uk/guidance/keeping-a-pet-pig-or-micropig>

"List of Things You Need For Your Mini Pig" Mom.me
<http://animals.mom.me/list-things-need-mini-pig-7834.html>

"Mini Pig Breeds" American Mini Pig Association
<http://americanminipigassociation.com/breeders/mini-pig-breeder-articles/mini-pig-breeds/>

"Mini Pig Pregnancy" MiniPigInfo.com
<http://www.minipiginfo.com/pig-pregnancy---what-to-expect-when-your-pig-is-expecting.html>

"Pig as Pets" RSPCA.org.uk
<https://www.rspca.org.uk/adviceandwelfare/farm/farmanimals/pigs>

"Pig Grooming Costs" FlyingPigGrooming.com
<http://www.flyingpiggrooming.com/>

"Pot Bellied Pig Pregnancy" Pigs4ever.com
<http://www.pigs4ever.com/pot_belly_pig_information/pregnancy.php>

"Review of Sexual Maturity in the MiniPig" NCBI.gov
<https://www.ncbi.nlm.nih.gov/pubmed/27102651>

"Socializing Mini Pigs" American Mini Pig Association
<http://americanminipigassociation.com/owners/helpful-owner-articles/socializing-mini-pigs/>

"Symptoms of UTI" American Mini Pig Association
<http://americanminipigassociation.com/mini-pig-education/mini-pig-health-care/symptoms-of-uti/>

"Vaccinations" American Mini Pig Association
<http://americanminipigassociation.com/mini-pig-education/caring-for-your-mini-pig/vaccinations/>

"What to Do in Case of Fever" American Mini Pig Association
<http://americanminipigassociation.com/mini-pig-education/mini-pig-health-care/what-to-do-in-case-of-fever/>

"Why We Feed A Raw Vegetarian Diet" PetitePorkers.com
<http://www.petiteporkers.com/feeding-potty-training-bathing--other-needed-care-of-your-piggy.html>

"Worming Your Pig" American Mini Pig Association
<http://americanminipigassociation.com/mini-pig-education/caring-for-your-mini-pig/worming-your-mini-pig/>

"Zoning Regulations – Legalize Mini Pigs" American Mini Pig Association
<http://americanminipigassociation.com/owners/ready-mini-pig-owner/zoning-regulations/>

Feeding Baby
Cynthia Cherry
978-1941070000

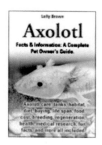

Axolotl
Lolly Brown
978-0989658430

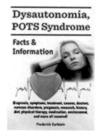

Dysautonomia, POTS
Syndrome
Frederick Earlstein
978-0989658485

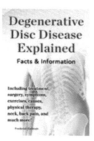

Degenerative Disc
Disease Explained
Frederick Earlstein
978-0989658485

Sinusitis, Hay Fever,
Allergic Rhinitis Explained
Frederick Earlstein
978-1941070024

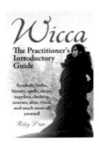

Wicca
Riley Star
978-1941070130

Zombie Apocalypse
Rex Cutty
978-1941070154

Capybara
Lolly Brown
978-1941070062

Eels As Pets
Lolly Brown
978-1941070167

Scabies and Lice Explained
Frederick Earlstein
978-1941070017

Saltwater Fish As Pets
Lolly Brown
978-0989658461

Torticollis Explained
Frederick Earlstein
978-1941070055

Kennel Cough
Lolly Brown
978-0989658409

Physiotherapist, Physical
Therapist
Christopher Wright
978-0989658492

Rats, Mice, and Dormice
As Pets
Lolly Brown
978-1941070079

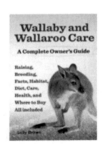

Wallaby and Wallaroo Care
Lolly Brown
978-1941070031

Bodybuilding Supplements
Explained
Jon Shelton
978-1941070239

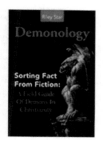

Demonology
Riley Star
978-19401070314

Pigeon Racing
Lolly Brown
978-1941070307

Dwarf Hamster
Lolly Brown
978-1941070390

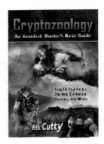

Cryptozoology
Rex Cutty
978-1941070406

Eye Strain
Frederick Earlstein
978-1941070369

Inez The Miniature Elephant
Asher Ray
978-1941070353

Vampire Apocalypse
Rex Cutty
978-1941070321

Made in the USA
Thornton, CO
07/23/23 17:10:50

c26ac52d-deab-4148-9806-e11723522059R01